The Care and Feeding
of Ministers

KATHLEEN NEILL NYBERG

The Care and Feeding

of Ministers

ABINGDON PRESS

NEW YORK
NASHVILLE

THE CARE AND FEEDING OF MINISTERS

Copyright © 1961 by Abingdon Press

Library of Congress Catalog Card Number: 61-7629

SET UP, PRINTED, AND BOUND BY THE
PARTHENON PRESS, AT NASHVILLE,
TENNESSEE, UNITED STATES OF AMERICA

To the one
who has so patiently endured
all my particular attempts
at *care* and *feeding*.

PREFACE

      Once the general public seemed quite content with cluckings of concern about the poor, dear minister's wife. The mood has changed. One can hear small stirrings of a movement getting under way to do something about her.

A scant twenty years ago important seminaries in this country considered married students a blight on the campus. A ministerial student who arrived at seminary in the married state was treated with distaste tinged with pity. Today he is lured by comfortable apartments and promises of baby sitters. The prevalence of wives on the seminary campus has not only made the minister's wife more visible but also more vulnerable. Vulnerable, that is, to scholarly scrutiny and the possibility of inspiring a set of rules designed to bring perfection to the parsonage.

Until this great rule book arrives, many amateurs may attempt to get in a few words of their own on the subject of caring for the clergy. Some of the more sanctimonious of this amateur advice causes otherwise fairly normal women to act perversely. This may be correctly construed as the inspiration for this small volume.

To reform one woman is miraculous; to reform many women is beyond the wildest of imagining. For women have a natural born resistance to rules and regulations—especially those which pertain to themselves. One can envision a rule book, no matter how scholarly and well documented, meeting with elaborate tactics of evasion. Yet many minister's wives are unhappy and dissatisfied in their relationship to their husband's work.

A woman will do the impossible to manifest her love for her husband. She wants desperately to express her affection in the care she proffers. She is often confused as to the best possible kind of care he needs. Perhaps if the minister's wife understood more profoundly the nature of her husband's life task she would be able to intelligently make changes in her own behavior which would improve the entire husband-wife relationship. It is hoped that the following chapters will stimulate thought and inspire young wives to seek continued understanding of both their husbands and the ministry to which they are committed.

It would be a comfort to think that the care and feeding of a minister was essentially equivalent to the similar needs of the baker or the plumber. But there are important and crucial differences. A minister's work spills over into his marriage, his home, and his affections. His wife is involved every day in many ways in his work. She can either be a part of the burden he must bear, or she has the inestimable privilege of making the burden seem lighter than it actually is.

There is no intention in these pages of answering the innumerable questions which ministers' wives are always asking about what to wear, when to appear and how, and how much work should she do in the church. Rather, it is the purpose of this book to suggest a way of relating to the entire task of the ministry, and to consider some ways in which specific behavior can add to or detract from that ministry. It will concentrate upon specific areas in which a wife is more involved and in which she can play an important and special role.

Being an involved and responsible minister's wife is a marvelous mixture of the sublime and the ridiculous, the solemn and the silly. If I chuckle when you prefer to cry, I ask your forgiveness. I write lightly of the things I love and cherish, as one jokes tenderly within the bonds of the family.

This book is addressed to young women who are anxious to, about to, or are married to men of the cloth. Should it fall into the hands of some tired parson, I beg his forbearance.

KATHLEEN NEILL NYBERG

ACKNOWLEDGMENTS

Many persons have aided and abetted the completion of this book. They may be quite unaware of making a contribution yet I feel a sense of gratitude to each of them. To the four ministers who hired me as secretary: Bert E. Smith, Arthur Rinkel, John E. Bowes and Seldon Humphrey. Each of these men allowed me the opportunity to know many ministers in various capacities, and to know the wives of ministers as well. I am especially grateful for the patient answers of my many friends to my constant barrage of inquiry regarding their attitudes toward the ministry. Rubbing elbows and hearts with countless ministers has been the joy of my life.

CONTENTS

CONTENTS

The Care and Feeding
of Ministers

1

the object of our affections

A minister is a man of finite limitations committed to a job of infinite dimensions. He has put his hand to God's plough and dares not look back. He accepts a call to a job which never can be finished and which expands as he matures. The more a man knows about the ministry the less confident he becomes of his ability to fulfill its demands. It is the most wonderful job in the world, and the most frustrating.

The ministry is undergoing tremendous transformation. Some of these changes are obvious while others cannot be detected by casual observation. A minister has a task which is at heart and core unchanging. Basically it is to confront man with God. This is changeless. Yet the means of accomplishing this task must constantly undergo re-evaluation. His approach to his job must be creative and open to change. As man and his world change, there is always the risk of getting out of touch with real men and the real God. There are two things a minister must know: where God is and where man is. This he cannot learn in seminary, tucking the information away for all time; he must be constantly alert. It is all too easy to shadowbox with ghosts and think it is the real thing.

Keeping in touch with God and with man is a moment-to-moment task. For while God is eternally changeless, and perhaps man is also changeless at the point of being in His image, yet all the paraphernalia of living beings in relation to each other and their living God shifts and changes without ceasing. The modern minister finds himself caught in a job which is already beyond human capacity to fully realize, and simultaneously in a position of having to constantly re-evaluate all aspects of the job as they relate to the basic purpose of his calling. He is somewhat in the position of a judge sitting under his own judgment.

Of course there are many men who are content to let well enough alone. They dismiss the struggle to understand their involvement as futile and time consuming. They get on with the job at hand. But the sensitive man wants more understanding and he is constantly seeking it.

All ministers need perspective, and perspective is hard to come by alone. This is one sound reason why ministers ought to marry. It was certainly not the reason why Martin Luther encouraged the clergy to marry. That great titan of the faith thought he was doing something for women. Of course he was. He was also doing a great deal for ministers. The formidable task of keeping alert, alive, fluid, and vital can be enhanced by love and marriage and the ensuing oneness, wholeness, and holiness of this experience. A minister without a good wife is like a woman without a mirror. He may be all there, quite intact, but he will lack an intimate portrait of himself reflected back from an outside source. Who needs to see himself as others see him more than a clergyman? This is not to suggest that a wife will make it her business to dissect or criticize his every move—she would not last long doing that. Some of this she must do. The knowledgeable minister will learn to see something of himself as he looks at his mate. He will see how she reflects the impact of his life on hers.

A minister is involved totally in his job. A doctor understands this kind of involvement. He knows what it is to be on call for twenty-four hours a day. Yet a physician enjoys a certain amount of freedom which is denied the minister. A doctor can go home and beat his wife if he has the desire and the strength to do so. He can also stop at the local bar or indulge in any other popular vice. His actions may provide some interested parties with gossip, but it is unlikely that his practice will suffer. If his private vice does not directly interfere with his effectiveness as a doctor, he will find acceptance in the community. The clergyman, however, knows better than anyone that everything he says, does, and thinks will directly affect his ministry. What he is in each moment contributes to the sum of his effectiveness. He is always both on call and on duty.

It would be naïve to give the impression that all men in the ministry yearn only for perfection in their calling. There are too many blatant examples of the contrary. There is a temptation to feel cynical at times. Many dark deeds have been committed under the cover of the cloak of church. Under the cloak of the great preacher may hide unencumbered ego-mania; under the cloak of great administrator may lurk power drive; under the cloak of wonderful counselor may dwell perverted eroticism. There are many ways to hide what needs and wills to be hidden. Temptations increase as success mounts. When a minister prays, "Lead us not into temptation," he is aware of the full meaning of this strange-sounding phrase. To help keep her minister from hiding, or of ever needing to hide, is in part the charge of the wife.

There are small and large occupational hazards on which the minister's wife learns to cry danger. The pitfalls are so plentiful primarily because the tasks are so magnificent. If one is frying an egg the failure hazard is small. But if one takes essentially the same ingredient and prepares a gourmet-style omelet, the failure possibilities are formidable. Success in the latter case is true accomplishment. So it is in the ministry. It is one thing to do a fried egg job and quite another to serve gourmet-style omelets. Most men will fail in some of the areas of this more complicated modern ministry. Much tender loving care will be required when such failure is unavoidable.

It is when failure threatens that many wives want to substitute affection with action. A wife has to do something when the man she loves faces danger. As her protective instincts mount, she may find herself lashing out at those who seem to be threatening her husband. However, a wife is not in a position to protect in direct combat. She is too closely identified with her husband in the minds of others. Her efforts appear to others as immature and self-righteous. Her most effective offensive is to remain quietly loving and affectionate.

The close identification of a minister and his wife often leads to confusion. A wife occasionally feels she is also the minister. She ought to remind herself frequently that there is only one minister in the family. It is important that a man feel total responsibility in his work. An aggressive wife can diminish a man's sense of accomplishment. A clergyman needs all the help he can get from others. The kind of assistance a wife can best give will be determined by her talents, interest, and personal need. The most important help she offers is uniquely hers: an undergirding of love and understanding.

There is a danger in speaking of ministers as a

group. We begin to feel there is some over-all pattern which, if known and adhered to, will guarantee a successful and happy ministry. Yet the ministry involves the whole person and is therefore subject to tremendous variation. A minister is defined in part by himself. As he is confined within a body, so his ministry is confined within his individuality. No amount of theological training or vocational gymnastics will alter this fact. To each his own is profoundly true.

Keeping this essential individuality in mind, we can still profit by comparing notes. For the individual minister is subjected to the limitations and demands of his environment. How he responds to these limitations may either improve or endanger his total ministry. A wife is part and parcel of this environment and it is her privilege and responsibility to fashion it in such a way as to give maximum fulfillment.

2

anybody home?

The center of operations for care and feeding of a minister is his home. He needs a warm home life to shelter him from the chill blasts of excessive demands upon his time and energy. It is his wife's privilege to preside over this private dwelling.

We have acknowledged the basis for discontent inherent in the pastor's calling. Smaller irritations clutter his daily round of activities. It is obvious that if he is to keep his sanity he will have to find a haven of rest and quiet. He must have a place where minimal demands are made upon him, and where he can be himself. His home and family can fulfill this need.

Much that is eloquent and sentimental has been written about family life. As a result, we are surprised to find that living in a family can be as difficult and demanding as it can be rewarding. The cost of creative family living is high in personal discipline and patience. It is worth the price. If a wife is unwilling to invest herself in her home she may find that it is no more than a way station in the husband's mind.

A common complaint of the wives of ministers is that their husbands are never home. When this is a regular condition, and not one confined to certain heavy seasons of the year, it is cause for alarm. A man's home ought to be the one place he can scarcely stay away from. When he is away, he yearns to be back in its warm embrace; when he is home, he begins to fill with eagerness for the job to do outside it. A good home is one which shelters and loves, but it also renews vigor and enthusiasm for the lifework.

What makes a man yearn for his home? Sometimes it is no more than to get in out of the rain. It can be that love is there. The pull which a wife and family exert on a man can be his greatest human assurance of security. When a man loves to come home it is usually because an affectionate and responsive wife is there. The minister's wife always has to struggle with herself and others to stay home. She is usually her own worst enemy. Her education may be against her. She is often trained to do a technical job which contributes practically nothing to the tasks of housewife and mother. The resulting frustration may cause her to be restless. To conquer this restlessness takes courage and persistence. But a home demands time and energy to produce contented members.

A minister's family can socialize itself out of existence. When the pivotal point of a family becomes church instead of home, it is time to reorganize.

Most clergy are eager to have families. Occasionally one meets a man who is hesitant to bring children into his world. He feels the disadvantages are too great. A minister's child is subjected to frequent uprootings; he can never say "this is home" of a particular place. He is put on the spot in much the same way as his father and mother; he has to get along on less fatherly attention than most other children. He endures the criticism of his elders for falling short of perfection; he is often castigated by his peers for his efforts at perfection. It would be irresponsible to deny the truth in these arguments. Yet they are only partial truth.

While the uprooting of a child may be difficult, it is the pattern rather than the exception. Transciency is as much a part of our culture as money. The heart of the problem is to provide security, basic and unassailable. A young pastor prepared to go into the mission field. He confided his greatest concern to be the upsetting of his family by so much moving. There would be over nine months of preparation involving several moves, plus a long ocean voyage and a strange land where no one spoke their language. Since his call was too urgent to ignore, he went ahead with his plans. He wrote back later that his children adjusted to their new life far better than he or his wife. The security of his children was in their mother and father. They did not need a place to call home. We owe our children this kind of security.

Are our children put on the spot too much? It is true they are seen and known by many people.

The shy child will resent this attention. The aggressive child may thrive on his special relationships. The average child tends to take or leave the attention as he wishes. Often it is the minister's family which is most guilty of making their children special. The term P.K. is seldom heard from laymen. If we seek to raise a special breed apart from the mainstream of youngsters, we are apt to influence lay people to think of them as different. No matter what previous patterns have been, we play a large part in making the world in which our children must live. It will be largely the attitude of the minister and his wife toward public attention which will most influence the attitude of their offspring.

The problem involving the lack of fatherly attention is primarily an individual matter. Some men can be excellent fathers with little effort; others have a struggle to show their affection. A young minister once told a friend that his father, who was also a minister, was never a private dad. He always thought of his father as his pastor. None of us would want our children to make this judgment of our efforts to be parents. Yet we all have a tendency to think that being a buddy to a boy is identical to being a good father. No amount of baseball, golf, or model building will suffice to make a dad. It takes more heart than time to make a father.

Once a child has his basic security he is ready for the occasional barb which comes his way simply because daddy is a minister. There is so much evidence that the children of parsonage homes enjoy a fuller life than the average, we ought to stop sympathizing and begin congratulating them on their good fortune.

The greatest hazard for the minister's child is that he may not be given enough room to rebel in. This is a child's inalienable right. It is especially hard to suffer our children's mistakes for they reflect upon our husband's ministry. Yet this is one of the risks one must take to raise normal children.

The sheltering of a minister from the stormy blasts, the nurturing of his children and the maturing of his marriage all take place in a house. Very likely this house will be called a parsonage, a manse, or a rectory. Whatever it is called, you can be sure it will offer some surprises. Parsonages come in all sizes, shapes, conditions, and colors. They are to be endured until a better plan comes along. Parsonages are currently undergoing widespread improvement. This is one area which is benefiting by the scarcity of clergy.

Much has been said and written for and against parsonages. You will from time to time in your life entertain some strong feelings about these houses in which you must live. It is a good thing to take care that this part of your life does not demand more of your total attention than it is worth. Basic acceptance will provide more serenity in the long view.

Beyond basic acceptance of each house for what little or much it is, we can concentrate our efforts on how we live in it and on what we bring along as our possessions. One minister and his wife made each parsonage strictly their own by painting the living room walls their private colors. They preferred white walls and a sky blue ceiling. Another collects antiques and finds that most parsonages make perfect settings for these objects. There is a parsonage where the living area is dominated by a lovely piano. In the corner there is a cello which always looks freshly played. There is not much else of beauty there, yet this home wears the imprint of its family. No matter how limited our resources we can find some things which express our love of beauty and our Christian joy.

It is important that we do not fall into patterns of acquisition for its own sake. Because the early years are often barren, we sometimes get bitten by the possession bug. The annoyance of going without is at times overwhelming. We tend to put too much importance on owning things. When we are prayerfully thoughtful about possessions, we know that we can only hold all things loosely. We dare possess with only the lightest touch. What we hold lightly cannot so easily grip us.

Whatever we make of our house, we must first of all keep it private. Before it is another thing, it is the private home of the minister. Parsonages can be tools to advance and enhance a man's ministry. He can share his home through entertaining in a way to inspire his people. Most people love to come to the minister's home; they enjoy feeling a part of his household. Yet we must remember, and help our parishioners remember, that the house is primarily our private home. It is not an extension of the church facilities.

Being gregarious creatures, ministers have a strong inclination to bring home stray dogs and people. Many parsonages become a cross between a hostelry and infirmary. There is a temptation to try to solve the acute problems of parishioners by bringing them into the shelter of our own homes. It sounds harsh to criticize such behavior. Yet we must think a long time before we invite others into our home to live, either for a short period or a longer time. When we invite the problems under our own roof which plague our husbands all day long, we are compounding his burden of concern. Ministers must learn to use many kinds of help available in the community. Surely they cannot hope to solve any great number of problems in such a personal manner. A minister may be better equipped and do a more thorough job if he safeguards his own home from the constant stream of problems which surround him.

Once we regard the parsonage as our private home, how shall we keep it? We have heard the advice that parsonages ought always to be presentable, in case someone drops in. This leads one to envision the perfect parsonage living room as sort of reception center. This is not a happy vision. Living causes disorder and if we are going to live in our houses, we are going to be upset most of the time. Cleanliness we must have; complete orderliness is too costly in terms of family comfort. A house which is lived in looks used. It is likely that the parishioner who drops in will be quite delighted to find that the minister and his family live normal lives.

Homes have personalities just as surely as do children. Houses tell stories about their occupants in much the same manner as youngsters reveal the truth about their parents. A minister's home often demonstrates the sermon more forcefully than words. Because this is so, a parsonage overflowing with love and tenderness will bless the whole congregation.

3

the eighty-hour week made easy

If there is a villian in the minister's story, his name is time. This villian can steal away a man's essential resources before he is mature enough to realize he has been victimized. While time is a precious possession for all men, it is especially dear to the minister.

A neophyte minister is ejected from the scholastic discipline into a life task which is largely self-motivated. He is the prime mover in almost every situation in the small local church. He is immediately thrown into a situation where he must discipline himself at every turn. He can no longer depend upon the exigencies of school to push and prod. Faced with the limitless range of ministerial tasks, he must determine how he will use his time in accomplishing them.

Young men come variously equipped for dealing with their time. Few realize the crucial importance of the early decisions. These early ways of doing things will very likely remain the life pattern. It takes tremendous effort to change once the habit has been practiced. Bad disciplines are heavy millstones. The increased use of the plan of internship is helpful, yet there comes a day when a man is on his own and his time is his own problem.

Some of the skills for using time wisely can be learned at the feet of another. The authentic teacher is experience. Fortunately the small churches where fresh seminarians try their wings come equipped with brotherly and patient parishioners. Surely these gentle folk must be destined to inherit special blessing in the beyond. It is through trial and error that the great lessons of how to use time are learned. No amount of book learning can possibly prepare a man for all the problems he will face in himself and others in his first parish.

Your minister will be fortunate if he is assigned to a charge which has a history and an organizational pattern. There is a tendency to send the untried young man to the blossoming young suburb to begin new work. These suburban churches have a strong appeal to the seminarian. Surely in such a situation one's fresh ideas will be accepted without a battle with what was done last year, or last century. A wife is also tempted with these situations, largely because they have new parsonages and attractive community facilities. Yet such a parish is a hazardous place for the young man who must set the pattern of his ministry.

The established church offers the young man a framework in which to plan his use of time. Frequently in the suburban development he must at once begin a building program. Any mature man who has endured the agonies of building a church knows the frightening demands on time, energy, and emotional resources it exacts. A young church is also in need of complete organizational planning. This need is complicated by untried leadership. There is limitless calling to be done, enough to take up his entire day. Yet he must preach, study, pray, begin some counseling, raise money and so much more. He will be faced with the practical considerations of how he will minister to his people through baptism, communion, weddings, and at funerals. Undoubtedly there are capable young men who can undertake such a job with out damaging the church or themselves. Most men need to begin at the beginning. The early years need to provide the atmosphere in which a minister can structure his own time and find his individual way.

A wife cannot do a great deal to help in the early discipline of time. She can, however, understand the great temptations he will face, and the painful necessity he faces each day of deciding priorities for his time. She must keep from becoming overanxious in areas where he is failing. A wife will often hear criticism of her husband's failings, many times in areas of which her husband seems unaware. She may feel it her duty to tell her husband what she has heard. If, however, the lack being criticized is a glaring one, chances are the husband is very aware of it. It is often the glaring omission which is never acknowledged even to a wife.

In the early years of marriage a wife is in a poor position to offer criticism, even of the second-hand variety. It may be that a wife is never in position to criticize. If a wife decides against criticism, she may decide on rationalization. It is an easy thing to excuse one's spouse of an inadequacy, especially in relation to the outsider. Many wives fortify their husband's excuses. This is safer than criticizing them.

When a wife senses that her husband is failing to use his time well, she may be tempted to fill in the gap herself. There was a wife who got her husband to do his calling by planning the calls and accompanying him. Another wife plans her husband's day from stem to stern. He follows her schedule and accomplishes a great deal. One hopes these are rare acceptions.

If a minister persists in misuse of his time, it is unlikely that any amount of criticism or help will improve the situation. There is a limitation of motivation and will power. Yet many ministers who have a lop-sided kind of approach are successful. They sometimes find a large church with a specialized ministry answers their particular problem.

While the patterns for use of his time are determined in the first parish, yet these patterns must change as the years go by. The mature man is often enmeshed in a large parish where time is at a premium. The demands far outweigh his resource of time. If he is not extremely careful he may allow the outside necessities to determine his use of time to the exclusion of his inner need.

The whole matter of time is complicated by certain popular myths widespread in this country. There is a quaint saying: "The minister only works on Sunday." There is considerable evidence that large numbers of people still think ministers loaf around the house, staying in bed until noon. They think a minister works on special occasions, such as weddings. And after all, a wedding takes only fifteen minutes and is fun! The public is becoming more aware that this is a false and vicious misconception. Yet a certain gulf exists between what a minister sees as the profitable use of his time and what the layman wants.

This is pointedly evident in the matter of study and sermon preparation. For most men sermon preparation has high priority and demands a large portion of time. The layman thinks of the sermon as easy and almost peripheral. The sermon is usually the focus of both attention and of criticism by the layman; yet he believes it deserves little time in preparation.

A famous English preacher was asked how much time he spent in sermon preparation. He answered:

"Practically none. I have an excellent classical education. A few moments for an outline is all I need." Unfortunately this man is a minority of almost one. Time for study and preparation is important and essential to the total ministry. Most ministers struggle with the awareness that time must be found for this study in spite of what laymen think.

The stewardship of time is more difficult than the stewardship of money. It is easier to see money and watch where it goes. You can grab hold of it and hang on if you must. Time, however, is spent in its moment of existence. It can't be saved, only spent. While it is momentary it can have rhythm and can be foreseen. It is especially difficult to achieve a rhythm of time in the ministry because the occupation is so filled with surprises. Many of these surprises we have to accept and incorporate into our lives. But when life is too full of unexpected interruptions, a minister becomes a frantic drifter. He flits from emergency to emergency without direction.

Many interruptions can be controlled or channeled. The essential problem is that most ministers welcome the interruption. If he is not extremely careful he can interrupt his whole life. There is a constant din of invitations to meetings, conferences, camps, social events, speaking engagements, and on and on. Many of these demands have an aura of excitement and challenge about them. They flatter a man's ego, and what is more, they are almost invariably good causes. Learning to sift the important from the trivial is an absolute necessity for a minister. It is just as crucial that he learns to separate the almost important from the most important. Obviously, a minister cannot do everything asked of him. He has to learn to concentrate first here, then there. The alternating of activity can help maintain perspective. This can refresh a man and save him from traveling in so deep a rut he can only see where he has been.

Rigidity in matters of time is to be avoided as assiduously as laxity. Some men look harried at the tender age of thirty. They never quite lose the appearance of being hounded by time. A minister has to learn to relinquish his plan for his time without rancor. A clergyman cannot afford a look of preoccupation when his work is interrupted by another person. There is nothing so deadly as seeking the help of someone who acts as though you are either a nuisance or bore. Some men get to look as though they are never quite able to hear anyone who is speaking to them. This is an advanced symptom of the time disease. The perfect minister ought to be able to give each person his undivided attention and time. To always have time for the loving relationships is both a great gift and a learned art. Preoccupation with time always shows. Worry about unfinished tasks becomes curtness with others, and even outright hostility.

Wives learn to guard their husband's time. This can be bane or blessing. Wives have been known to chant: "He is so tired, he works so hard, he won't rest, he hasn't time for lunch, and so on." All of this may be true, yet a wife does her husband more damage than help with this sort of dirge. Occasionally she may allow herself this acknowledgement in public, but if it becomes a primary topic of her conversation it is disastrous. Such a chant may in fact reflect diverted nagging. A wife may be covering up her sense of being neglected by her husband by publishing his busyness abroad. It is easy to feel neglected when you are the wife of a minister. His preoccupations are so omnipresent that many women feel they do not exist for their husbands. There are times when all ministers are preoccupied to the extent that they are not very good husbands. If this attitude becomes the rule rather than the exception, its roots are deep and may require drastic measures to eliminate.

When a minister shuts the office door at night,

he does not shut his work behind it. Yet to survive a minister must learn to lay down one matter and pick up another, giving each attention and time in its turn. Wives can help by giving their own undivided attention to home and husband. A wife can make the home a haven of rest for a weary soul rather than an extention of the church. Sometimes she has to sacrifice knowledge about all the details of the church life. A husband deserves respite from thinking about and reliving all these details when he is at home. She can have interests outside the church work so that her own thinking is not totally enmeshed in the same problems as her husband faces.

When a minister is obviously overworked, a wife thinks longingly about the day when he will be in a church with a large enough staff to relieve him of much detail. This might be called the staff myth. It enjoys a wide coterie of believers. If the day comes when your minister has a staff of more than a part-time janitor and volunteer secretary, he is in for some rude surprises. Few administrative problems are as time consuming as staff relationships. When there is a staff the administrative tasks have a dimension which increases in proportion to the number employed. Staff is not pie in the sky by and by. It is exhausting and time consuming.

Yet the eighty-hour week can be endured and even enjoyed. A minister can learn to live with his work because it is a total life commitment. He is pressured from without but also from within. He learns to live with long hours by basic structuring of his time so that unfinished tasks remain at a minimum. He learns alternation of activity. He learns to relax within the framework of the job in a renewing way. More than this, he has the unlimited resources of the Almighty working when he works, but also working when he fails.

4

fact and fancy about friends

An unwritten law insists that ministers and their wives should not have intimate friends among their parishioners. This law meets with considerable difficulty: many accept it, few follow it. There are reasons and rationalizations which make the rule unworkable in the everyday world. This is apparently the kind of thing one believes in, advises others to follow, then fails to follow oneself. Good intentions to obey its precept bow to human frailty with astonishing regularity.

Rationalization begins with the definition of intimate. Some clergy do not know the distinction between intimate and friendly. For fear of being overly intimate some ministers become cold, aloof, and withdrawn. Others cannot draw the line: warmth and friendliness spill over into intimacy with some parishioners. Either of these attitudes can restrict a man's effectiveness in the ministry. A definition of intimate is: a relationship to a person which involves entertaining and being entertained in a social way with frequency.

The justification for believing a minister ought not to become intimate with certain parishioners is sound. A minister must relate to many people, usually hundreds. No man is capable of intimate contact with so many persons, therefore he is faced with the necessity of deciding who will be his special friends. This is the initial hazard. Those who are not included for this special relationship may show signs of open or latent jealousy. "Why doesn't that minister like us as well as he does the Smiths?" This is not a comfortable question to answer. The person who is jealous is difficult to work with, and sometimes dangerous.

Parishioners are wary of the minister's special friends. They suspect that the clergyman shares his confidences with his cronies. Truth to the contrary, suspicion mounts.

The most serious consideration involves the friends themselves. For a minister sacrifices the noninvolved relationship so necessary to his pastoral responsibility. When his special friends are in trouble, he simply cannot function as their minister in the way he ought. They are in fact deprived the privilege of a pastor when he is most needed in their own lives. This is a precious price to pay for friendship.

Too many persons may demand a friend relationship to the pastor. Once a minister allows himself very special friends, he must not deny this privilege to others who seek it. There may result a draining away of vital resources of energy and time to satisfy the demand for his friendship. Some ministers are caught up in such a round of social activity that their work suffers. They also abdicate family life to their wife. Getting in those extra golf games, handball sessions, fishing excursions, hunting expeditions, and on and on, will take its toll. Even when the family is included on such excursions the result is not equivalent to time spent with just the family. It does not make sense to sacrifice one's private family life on the altar of friendship.

A final consideration is the least important and deserves only passing mention. It is the unwisely chosen friend. Is there any more potentially dangerous enemy than a disenchanted friend? No matter how pure one's life and work is, it is possible for a bitter person to corrupt it.

If, finally, we are convinced that it is unwise for a minister and his wife to have special friends in the congregation, where will friends be found? Other ministers in the community are logical targets for our friendship. Common interests have a tendency to result in constant shoptalk. A minister needs friends among his fellow clergy, but he also needs to know men in other fields, of other faiths and interests. It will take effort to find these friends and to nourish these relationships.

When the parsonage family prepares their annual budget, an item ought to read "For Making Friends." Frequently a minister will feel that he cannot afford to entertain in his home for other than church purposes. But this item is not a luxury, it is a necessity. The opportunities for making friends are limitless. Clergymen are invited more places to meet more people than a politician. It is important to learn how to make these opportunities for friendship flower into reality.

An excellent way to make a friend is to invite him into the intimate atmosphere of one's home. In the early, lean years of the ministry, one has to learn how to entertain with simplicity. Essentially it is the wife's responsibility to make the home an inviting place for outsiders. She can make her home a place that is fun to be in. This quality is not measured by elegance or elaborate tools for entertaining. The house which is fun to visit gives the guest a sense of being wanted, included in the life of the family, and enjoyment of a relaxed atmosphere.

All this is not to say that one's church people are to be cut off from friendly relationships. All ministers have the privilege of relating to people in a warm and wonderful way. A pastor is with his people during the difficult and the happy life-shaping experiences. Deep and penetrating bonds of affection are forged which can never be broken. An overflow of gratitude and love surround a minister and his family, far too precious to be described in mere words. There is a crucial difference in the manner in which a minister responds to this kind of affection and how he responds to those who seek him as a personal friend. It is the difference between loving acceptance of friendliness and initiating friendship.

A simple illustration is the dinner invitation from the parishioner. Such an invitation is a delightful experience and greatly enjoyed. It does not require a return invitation to the parsonage. The proper response is a warm personal thank-you either in a phone call or note. An invitation to dinner at the parsonage many times initiates an unwanted round of dinners. It is difficult to be on the receiving end of much gracious hospitality without responding in kind. A minister learns to express his thankfulness in other ways.

There are times for extending special friendliness beyond the call of duty. These times will become obvious with experience. When tragedy strikes in the parish, the minister is ready to invite the sorrowing family into his home. In such cases one is not being choosey, but one is being willing to serve anyone in such need.

The ethical considerations of personal friendships go beyond private preference. Ministers seldom serve in the same parish forever. They tend to have successors. If a pastor makes a collection of personal social friends in his church he cannot drop them when he is moved. The interchange of relationships necessary to nurture close friendship will be continued to some extent. It is scarcely human to expect either a minister or a parishioner to relinquish a personal friendship just because they are separated. This is not emotionally feasible. Unnecessary hardship is inherited by the successor.

Any minister who serves a parish where the former pastor cannot break his intimate ties knows the sorrow which is reaped. It is quite impossible for the former minister's special friends to completely accept their new pastor without feeling disloyal to an old friend. They may make all the motions of acceptance, yet most fail. How can they, when their loyalty is placed elsewhere? There has occurred a subtle displacement of loyalty from the Church of Jesus Christ to a particular minister. There are rare individuals who are capable of fully accepting each minister as a personal friend with equal loyalty. Yet these persons are few. Also there are those who were close friends of one pastor and demand a similar relationship to the next minister. Should he feel such intimate friendships are unwise, he is considered cold and unfriendly.

Ministers often hear: "We have invited Pastor X back to marry our daughter. He is a close family friend." There is heartache to be endured in these cases. Although the unwritten ethics of the ministry state that a former minister does not come back for such events as weddings and funerals without first consulting the present pastor, this is not enough. To obey the letter of the law does not solve the problem. There remains the conundrum of the minister who can scarcely refuse such a request without appearing officious or selfish. Baptisms, weddings, funerals are the rightful province of the minister in charge. They are also crucial to his ministry. These are the occasions of depth in which the church ministers to man's need at a time when he is willing to be moved. They are too precious to be abdicated to any other. It is up to Pastor X to decide he will not return to his old parish, even though he is invited through the present pastor. When Pastor X is tempted to return he should ask himself whether he wants his predecessor ministering among his own people. This is usually a sobering reminder.

This has been addressed to those of good intention. There are pastors who use friendship for their own miserable purposes. A few individuals make a veritable business of gaining personal friends for the express purpose of placing them in strategic offices in the church. Such a minister then rides confidently upon the backs of his friends without fear of a murmur of discontent. There is little to be done about such unscrupulous individuals. All ministers have to be constantly alert to the temptation arising within themselves to follow this same pattern.

No one in his right mind could call these considerations of the problems of friendships academic. They are as real as bread, butter, and germs. Ministers and their wives want and need intimate friends. For many inner security depends upon the number and warmth of such associations. But ministers need a portable security. Just as we feel we are being comforted by a warm blanket of love, we may discover we have cuddled up to a furry monster. In this area of a minister's life, his decision must be realistic, workable, and consistent. This is a great deal to ask of any human decision.

Here are some questions which ministers can ask themselves on occasion to clarify their own thinking in matters of friends:

Are you seeking personal friendships in your parish for your own sense of security?

Are you in fact cutting off such friends from other lay people in your church by setting them apart in a special relationship?

Are you using special friends to get your way in the church?

What would happen if you found it necessary

to restrain such friendship—might you lose a
parishioner?

Can you break this tie with understanding
when you leave this parish?

This is an area of our church life which deserves frequent and honest evaluation. A consistent attitude, arrived at with objectivity, can
save a minister many heartaches.

5

a chicken for the Sabbath pot

A gnarled old man accompanied by a loud yell burst into the parsonage door. It was six o'clock in the morning on the first day in the new parish. The early visitor threw an unceremoniously wrapped chicken, feathers and all, into the sink. This was one minister's first gift. Caught unawares and not quite awake, he muttered his first thank-you. This minister found this was the beginning of a long series of love offerings which were to come his way.

This particular farmer was a frequent and welcome visitor to that parsonage. His gifts were a joy to receive. When the gift was a bag of potatoes, he would yell that they were rotting anyway. When the gift happened to be a chicken, he invariably stated that she was about to die of old age. The eggs he brought were always, to hear him tell it, fit only for pigs. The melons were of such a poor quality he could not sell them in the market. Of course, he had brought the minister the choicest of everything. But this simple man intuited what many sophisticated people never learn: accepting gifts can be a difficult experience. It is more blessed to give than to receive; but it is also easier to give than to receive.

Every minister and his wife need to learn the art of accepting gifts in such a loving way that each gift is twice blessed. A gift without a giver may be bare; a gift without a grateful recipient is desolate. There is no more crushing experience than to give someone a gift which you feel is special, only to have the recipient mumble a subdued, unenthusiastic thanks. It is important to know how to receive a gift in such a way as to enrich the giver. This is easier said than done.

Gifts come to the parsonage for various reasons. The farmer's gifts of food came in part because he knew the minister needed this to supplement his small salary. Ministers inherit a long tradition of receiving goods for services. Many of the older generation remember what grandmother did, and mother did, and so they do it. One thanks God that previous generations did remember the minister with a portion of the crop, or many would have perished. While we no longer live in a barter society, the old patterns linger.

Gifts come to the minister as a gesture of gratitude for some special service he has rendered. They also come to express love and affection in the outward symbol. But gifts also come from those who enjoy the feeling of the pastor's dependency upon their generosity. Gifts are given out of guilt, for appeasement, apology, and occasionally because a gift is easier given than "I'm sorry" is said. Gifts obviously arise out of guilt or triumph. For these reasons, the gift bearer might be compared to the prayermaker. Prayers certainly come to God from all sorts and conditions of men. We are confident that God receives all prayers. The fruit of each prayer differs and is conditioned in part by the circumstances and motives of the prayermaker. If we dare for a moment see ourselves as accepting gifts in the similar spirit in which God receives prayers, we may gain some illumination. We must receive, then, the gifts of each person equally, without any sense of rejection, no matter how demeaning we may feel the gift is intended to be. Then we trust in the knowledge that good motivation will bear its good fruit; that questionable motivation may be redeemed through our loving acceptance of the gift and the giver.

Not only individuals give gifts to a minister. Occasionally the church family will also give a gift. These church gifts vary all the way from leftover flowers from the altar to new cars and trips to Europe. Such gifts are wonderful to receive, especially if they are not in lieu of cash salary. They give the parsonage family a sense of being wanted and appreciated. However, they are often sources of great distress to a pastor. Churches are seldom consistent. A minister who receives a gift one Christmas and not the next asks himself if this means he is less wanted. He wonders how a church can love him one season and despise him the next. It is only human to be puzzled by this behavior on the part of a congregation. It helps a little to understand that a church is not a cohesive, consistent entity capable of acting with as much discipline as an individual. In almost all churches, with the possible exception of highly organized ones, such matters are at the mercy of the individuals who are in a particular job at a specific moment. The church temporal is made up of an assortment of individuals of all degrees of stability and responsibility, as well as imagination, in these matters. The leadership is expected to be constantly shifting. The tender personal relationship of a pastor and congregation is forever at the mercy of the powers that be.

Whenever we speak of the church relating to the pastor, we must remember it is actually individual church members relating to him. The individuals who bear the responsibility do not necessarily reflect the sentiments of the majority of the church members. One young minister's wife gave birth to her first child while her husband was a pastor of a small city church. The church failed to acknowledge this birth with so much as a card of congratulation. The hurt which this wife sustained at this rebuff has colored and impaired her relationship in all her husband's churches through the years. She is convinced that no church cares the least bit about either her family or herself. Her intelligent mind tells her that she is wrong in her feeling, but her heart will not be convinced.

On the other hand, the gifts given by a congregation can buoy up tired spirits. One pastor received a gift of cash with this note attached: "I was chosen to pick a gift for you and the Mrs. from the church family. I decided on a lamp but since my taste is so old hat and yours is garishly modern, it is going to be up to you. Get one you will love and we will all put up with. With affection . . ." It is obvious that the imagination of the individual made this gift so special. Very few of us know how to give a good gift; we should not be surprised when the church fails.

Many laymen and a few ministers are under the impression that ministers are constantly receiving gifts of moment. This is a gross exaggeration. Gifts come to a pastor in haphazard fashion. Many churches never give the pastor a gift. But whatever and whenever they come, we have the privilege of receiving them in love.

Gift receiving is but half the question; what about gift giving? What are you and your husband to do about giving gifts? Contemplate for a moment the hundreds of weddings to which you will be invited, the baptisms, the birthdays you will share, the graduations and anniversaries. It is the pastor's great privilege to share in these occasions. How shall you relate to these events? Just like everyone else? Will you give a gift as is the custom? Will you settle on a token gift and give the same to all? Will you give only to church members? Only when you are formally invited? Or will you give gifts only to families who habitually give gifts to your own family?

Experience is the best teacher in answering such questions. The difficulty is one needs the answer at the time of the first wedding in the first parish. There have been various answers given to these questions. Whatever you may chose as your solution there is one cardinal rule which must be followed: be absolutely consistent. Many pastors decide that they must not give gifts to parishioners. Experience has proved this to be one good solution. It is not an easy policy to follow. There are many times when a pastor and his wife would love to give a gift to someone special. But once a rule is broken in this regard, there will be unhappy consequences. There is no news which travels so rapidly as a pastor's gift to a parishioner. The most circumspect laymen cannot resist the mention that "this is from the minister." Unless one has an adequate answer for all the others who have not received a special gift, one is in for criticism justly earned.

Some ministers decide to give gifts. It is financially a burden at the outset and remains a burden. Usually as the salary increases, so does the congregation and resultant obligations. One minister returned a gift to each person from whom he received a Christmas gift. When he moved into another parish, he found his former parishioners continued the practice of a gift at Christmas. He did likewise. After a number of parishes, he is burdened with the necessity of preparing the entire year for the Christmas deadline. This kind of situation ceases to be a joy. Forty years in the pastorate can accumulate a great deal of involvement. This man enjoys very much the sense of being remembered by many people that the gift giving symbolizes. Must he not also feel a deep sense of frustration, perhaps even resentment, for the precious time and energy stolen both from his current parish and his family to fulfill these personal obligations? One wonders.

We make a choice in this matter as in every other area of our lives: what is going to have priority on our time, attention, and money?

If a minister decides to give gifts to his parishioners, he must be careful not to embarrass them. A layman might be caught up in a round of gifts which he neither enjoys nor desires. When a minister receives a gratuity for performing a wedding ceremony, and he also gives a personal gift, he may leave the parishioner in a quandary. Functioning in his capacity as clergyman he is on the giving side of the equation; the parishioner is on the receiving. The layman ought to be able to express his gratitude without feeling uneasy.

To decide not to give gifts may imperil the soul. To be always on the receiving end is to place oneself in a dangerous position. One safeguard is to be generous in other ways. Perhaps the minister will decide a tithe is not enough for him. It would be disastrous to decide never to give gifts if it simply meant more for himself.

A minister can rightly express his generosity in relation to other persons on the church staff. Frequently the minister will be remembered with a church gift while the rest of the staff goes unnoticed. A minister can remember his staff in those special ways which warm the heart.

Learning how to give the good gift, and how to receive the generosity of others in love, is an art to be learned. For the parsonage family it is more than an art, it is a crucial ingredient of life which can either cripple or enhance its total impact on a community.

6

the evil root bears
beautiful blossoms

The evil root which bears such beautiful blossoms often has incredibly bitter fruit. Money is no laughing matter to a minister. Almost without exception our ministers need tender love and affection in matters of money. Preachers are overly sensitive about their incomes, and not without cause. It is no secret that they are underpaid and overworked—a combination not likely to generate peace of mind in money matters. Having acknowledged this, one also has to say that higher salaries and shorter work weeks would not solve the eternal problem of man and his money.

It is not by chance that the teachings of Jesus are constantly concerned with money and possessions. Money is the symbolic manifestation of a man's inner condition. "Where a man's treasure is, there is his heart also." In some ministers' homes the constant shortage of enough income is such a corrosive factor in the family, the result is a preoccupation with it. When one is hungry one thinks primarily about food; when one is broke, one thinks about money.

The fact that inadequate incomes so corrode a minister's family life makes ironic the attitude of many laymen toward salaries. Some laymen say, "Keep the minister's salary low and you keep him humble." Evidence is that low salaries do not breed humility, they breed humiliation. The layman has forgotten that it is not what goes into a man's life from the outside which corrupts him, rather what proceeds from him. Ministers would be under a greater challenge to practice true humility if their salaries were comparable to other professional men. To have the option of what one would do with abundance is a true test of a man's mettle.

But this is idle fancy. Most ministers will have to live on minimum incomes. There is a strange truth to learn about money: it can bless or curse those who possess it. The amount of money a man accumulates is quite irrelevant. The pauper and the prince both have to answer the same questions of stewardship. Only when we know that all we have belongs to God can we be enriched by money. If we forget our stewardship no amount of money can save us from impoverishment. Likewise we can be blessed plentifully while carrying a very thin purse.

There is a temptation when one is involved totally in church work to feel that everything we have and do is being given back to God. This is a temptation because it leads some clergy to feel that they do not need to make a cash contribution to the church. The first claim upon the minister's budget, as it is upon anyone else's budget, is God's tithe. This is not to say that ministers are not generous. They are usually generous to a fault. They will give away their shirts if not watched. A generous heart is part of basic working equipment in the ministry. Yet giving must not be left to casual contribution. Giving must become a built-in discipline in our minds as well as in our hearts.

Ostentation is unforgiveable. A minister has to remember to forget what his left hand is doing in these matters. We may convince ourselves that our giving in a noticeable way will influence others to be generous. We can be sure parishioners will be impressed by such public demonstration. We must ask ourselves the embarrassing question concerning how pure our motivation was.

As to what is left after the initial gift to God's work, it will require careful planning to cover necessary expenses. There are many places to obtain professional help in budgeting. We are sometimes loathe to seek such help. We hate to admit our need. Yet why should we think ourselves experts in everything; we are lucky to be an expert in something.

There are always a few persons in every profession who embarrass the many. A minority of ministers has found it inconvenient to meet financial obligations. As a result, many communities have the opinion that ministers are poor credit risks. Since the world is full of small-minded persons eager to give the ministry a bad name, the minister who acts like a parasite is grist for their gossip mill. Failure on the part of the few affects the reputation of the majority who are meticulous about bill paying.

Most ministers are excellent credit risks. Perhaps too good for their own sake. It is so easy to buy on credit that many clergy owe far too much. It is a good plan to sit down once a year and add up all moneys owed and saved. It can be a sobering experience.

A financial factor in the pastor's life which is not always recognized either by the laity or the clergy is that the salary represented by the parsonage is lost to the future. A minister does not have the option of what he is going to do with a large portion of potential salary. He is unable to build equity in a home. While the average layman may be further in debt than the average clergyman, he is nevertheless building equity for his future. His debt is usually his mortgaged home. This is one of the unrealized unfairnesses of the parsonage plan. The budget must always take into account saving for a home for retirement.

It is good stewardship to keep sound financial records in the home. This is one job which a wife can take over. That is, unless she cannot manage to handle the money in a business-like manner. It is just as poor stewardship to spend too much time and energy on money matters.

When a scarcity of money is a constant worry, it may also become the chief topic of conversation. The subject manages to come up in many ways, not only at home but in groups of people. This is not to assert that worldly possessions are not worthy of conversation; it is to remind us that preoccupation with money can interfere with one's effectiveness in the ministry.

The matter of gratuities has come under scrutiny during the past few years. Increasingly ministers are refusing to accept personal fees for the special services of the church. If they do accept them at all, it is with the explanation that the money will be placed in a special fund for use in needed ways. The use to which such funds have been dedicated varies from the purchase of equipment for the church or parsonage, to loan funds for needy persons. One minister remarked that he didn't dare think of his fund as for loans for the needy—he was the needy person he kept thinking of!

The reasons for this trend away from personal fees are, of course, varied. One obvious reason is the danger of having lay people feel they "pay" for such gifts of grace as baptism or the Christian funeral. Such functions are an integral part of the total ministry and as such are no more to be paid for in a special way than is the Sabbath sermon.

There is felt a need to allow gratefulness to be expressed at times of special services, especially for those who are not members of the church. Yet when the gift is accepted for the church or a special fund, the nonmember finds he is thanking the church rather than an individual minister.

There is a sense in which the fee may demean the ministry. This is especially obvious in the practices associated with weddings in our culture. The place of the minister in this important event (and therefore, the place of the church which he represents) is the last financial consideration. He usually receives less money than has been spent for the bride's bouquet. If the services of the church are thought to be so insignificant as is indicated by their financial consideration, then the ministry is failing to rightly inform the parishioner. If the services of the church are truly priceless, then a minister should refuse to allow a price tag to be put upon them.

Gratuities may do the ministry continuing damage from an entirely different point of view. By and large laymen think a minister receives a great deal of money in fees. This is used time again to justify low salaries. Certainly an unpredictable ten, fifteen, or fifty dollars are not worth the sacrifice of a more realistic consideration of salary.

And we do have to be concerned about salaries. Most ministers shrink away from the open discussion of the salary. Yet the silence of the minister may cause practices to continue which are harmful to both the minister and the layman. Salaries are important in our day as they have never been before. A man is measured by the size of his salary in the eyes of the world—and, after all, this is where ministers are working. Ministers can despise this fact, regret it, disavow it, yet it remains a fact of life. As a result, the ministry has been steadily declining in status in the secular world. For the sake of the world, if not for the comfort of the minister, clergymen ought to be paid very well indeed. This is just as true in the teaching profession. When one studies salaries in America one gets the impression that the important jobs are in business, science, and medicine. Education, government, and the church, if judged by their price tag, are of relative minor importance to our culture.

Whenever the subject is raised, there is a hue and cry about dedication. It is argued that if ministers are highly paid the profession will attract status seekers rather than dedicated men. There are checks and balances in this regard. It is highly unlikely that a status seeker will endure long the pressures necessary to fulfill the demands of the modern church. As a matter of fact, dedication to the job is quite irrelevant to salary.

The subject of money in the church has all the explosive qualities of dynamite wrapped in glycerin. Whenever a good fight rages it is usually about money. For this reason ministers are timid about raising the subject of money in relation to salary. Yet each man has some responsibility to educate his congregation in this regard. There is a most irrational attitude toward ministers' incomes among laymen. One extreme illustration is the church where the pastoral committee was discussing the ensuing year's salary. One man protested a suggested raise of two hundred dollars on the basis that the minister was out for all he could get. This particular layman netted an income over twenty-five thousand dollars each year; the pastor's salary was two thousand dollars. Sometimes it is the people who live most comfortably themselves who are the most dedicated to keeping the minister uncomfortable.

A minister is greatly blessed if he can take money or leave it. The gospel does not teach us to despise money, but to be master over it. If a minister can admit with honest zest that he likes money, yet with the same zestiness know that he can get along without it if he has to, he has achieved maturity in money matters.

Regardless of how mature a minister is in matters of money, he may still suffer some pangs about it. It is a melancholy thing for man to be at his prime and yet earn a salary no larger than that of a novice engineer. A clergyman often feels that he is doing an injustice to his family, to his children's future. A wife can help alleviate these feelings by keeping her demands reasonable and encouraging her children to do likewise. Care never ends in this matter of money. It varies greatly according to the individuals, but the basic approach can always be the same: we are God's stewards whether we deal in pennies or in great sums.

7

how to live with other people's problems

The subject of a minister and his confidences is approached with fear and trembling. It is in many ways as touchy a subject as the matter of personal friends among the parishioners. It too is the kind of thing one believes others should be concerned about, but not oneself. Yet the sharing or not sharing of a husband's secrets can be the most explosive element in a minister's life. It deserves our honest attention.

There is a strong consensus of opinion among experienced clergy that the confidences placed in the hands of a minister are his alone. This procedure is intellectually and morally sound; it is emotionally all but untenable for some wives. The plaint so frequently heard by ministers from their wives, "I don't know anything about anything" ought to become a happy theme song. This is one area of parsonage life where ignorance abounds with bliss.

During the half-glow, half-tension phase of early marriage, a wife is armed with a powerful argument for knowing her husband's confidences. She argues that a sound marriage is based on mutual sharing, nothing held back. Chances are that the bridegroom will respond to some degree to this appealing plea. It is a romantic but impractical basis for sharing other people's confidences. The neophyte minister is the most prone to succumb to his wife's wishes for he has so little to share and is probably eager to talk it over with someone anyway.

In these early years a wife may not be able to resist the temptation to pump her husband for his special knowledge of people and things. If he does not maintain silence in these matters, two rules must be observed with infinite care. First, the husband must tell no one else. Second, the wife must tell no one. At all costs in personal discipline absolute secrecy must be maintained at all times and in all places. A once-revealed confidence is easily repeated; once a secret has been verbalized it can be spoken again with little effort.

There is only one thing worse than a minister's wife who goes around repeating everything she knows and even that which she shouldn't know: a minister who can't keep a confidence. The layman is always on guard for such lapses. He has every right to be deeply concerned at this point.

There are appropriate exceptions which become obvious. If a minister needs expert advice on a particular problem from another man of more experience, he certainly must relate the essentials of the case. There is one simple, sure safeguard. He never needs to reveal the name of his confidante. The name of the person is essentially irrelevant to the problem. This applies also when a minister would like to verbalize a problem with his wife. The wife does not need to know the identity of the person about which he speaks to offer what insight she might have. When we are praying for others, even about specific problems, we do not need to know the identity of the individual concerned, for God knows.

The word disaster is not too strong a term to use in describing the results of indiscretion in this area of our church life. There is the possibility of getting involved in some dramatic episode in which an indignant parishioner accuses either the wife or husband of revealing a confidence. Usually indiscretion will cause a less dramatic and more insidious kind of disaster. The quiet and insistent word is passed that the minister is not a trustworthy person. The days of his personal counseling are numbered in the particular community in which this happens. This is tragic enough, although it is only part of the story. News concerning ministers travels at the speed of sound, especially bad news. A poorly kept confidence may result in a crippling of a man's ministry for years. A slip of the tongue has haunted many a minister wherever he has gone. Someone always knows someone, or has an Aunt Clara, in the next parish. Living down a past mistake, or escaping from it, is a task of dimensions which overwhelm us. Our past pursues us to the grave. This is a most unpleasant thought, but like many unpleasant things, it is worth knowing.

When a wife desires to know her husband's confidences, she is certain she would die before she would repeat a word. Yet she must consider the scrutiny of others beyond the spoken word. If she knows a shocking secret in which a specific parishioner is involved, how much of that confidence is revealed in her voice, her facial expression, or her eyes? Perhaps she feels moral revulsion at the knowledge she possesses. Can she be sure it is not showing? Or she may be moved to such tender sympathy that her special feelings will be apparent to another. If a wife is not a sphinx, she will want to respond without worrying about what is showing to everyone. If her source of information is from public sources, she is able to act naturally and reveal all the love she feels.

A minister's wife should wear her heart on her sleeve. This is her most attractive item of attire. It deserves to be worn in a pure and unfettered condition.

There are types of information about parishioners which a wife must know in order to act intelligently toward them. Also if there exists a situation in which a wife must be a direct help, she will need to know the confidence. Usually she requires just enough information to avoid doing any damage. It may be wise for a wife to know the names of persons who are under special stress without knowing the specific problem. In this event, she can use care in approaching these individuals to do certain church tasks. There is a constant need for caution, however, for good intentions do not always strike upset people in a positive way. The more involved an individual is in a disturbing personal problem, the more easy it is to offend him. A minister's wife has to be very careful not to give special attentions to distraught people. These attentions had better come from the minister.

It is an agonizing experience for any woman to be so near and yet so far from so much interesting information. Whether it is described as female curiosity or loving interest in others, women like to know details of other people's lives. It is easy to seek one's thought-food at the table of others. The frustrated wife often focuses upon the problems of parishioners as a cover for not facing her own. If her curiosity drives her to plague her husband with a barrage of questions, she needs to examine her own life more intently. A personally disturbed wife will sometimes probe others on her own time for information about their lives. This is usually a clear sign that it is not the lives of others which needs attention so much as her own.

About now, someone is sure to be discouraged because the fundamental cause of probing by wives for confidential information has been ignored. The most obvious motivation for wanting to know what goes on behind the study door is jealousy. Seeing a husband constantly closeted with other women, sharing their innermost secrets, is not easy for any minister's wife. Most learn to live with it. The problem of severe jealousy is a matter needing professional help, and quickly. The problem of jealousy cannot be met by pat advice or statistics about the experience of others. Nothing is relevant to a jealous woman except her jealousy.

A minor skirmish now and then with jealousy is to be expected. A quick defensive action here and there will be necessary. If a wife has the fundamental conviction that she must respect the sacred trust another imparts to her husband, she will have the battle of jealousy half won. If she will often place herself in the position of the confidante, she will realize how important it is that her husband does not repeat the secrets of others.

Even if it were conceded that the perfect wife could keep every confidence, there is a more important consideration. As a minister matures and his responsibilities expand, it will become an impossible burden for him to share all that happens in his work. If he does, he will be spending many hours retraveling tedious and tense terrain. It seems an unnecessary burden to cause a tired husband to relive much that is unpleasant when he finally finds time to relax. The wife might better spend her time helping him to unclutter his mind of such problems. If a minister and his wife spend their time together wandering through the labyrinthine trails of the moral and spiritual problems of others, they will lose precious time belonging to their private lives.

8

pruning and grooming

A preponderance of the work of a minister is performed in the sitting position. Often the sitting is combined with eating. There are innumerable luncheons, dinners, banquets, teas, and parishers armed with coffee pots and delicious deserts. The hazards of excessive sitting and eating tend to obviate themselves as the years roll by. A wife may have to become aggressive in the area of consumption to keep her husband healthy and in shape.

Since she can do the most direct good in the home, she will begin early the art of cooking nourishing, low calorie meals. She will begin this program long before the danger signs appear. The clean plate virtue of the child may undo the mature male: it is habit forming to eat more than is necessary for health. A minister cannot afford to carry around excess poundage. The wear and tear of these pounds will take its toll. He also cannot afford to be excessively thin for his job demands a horde of energy and endurance. There are aesthetic reasons as well for avoiding overweight which should not be ignored. A minister who is overweight from overeating may advertise his inability to control his appetites.

An important determining factor in food consumption is one's attitude toward it. Each individual relates to eating in a different way. Many Americans seem to consume food in great quantities as part of a consuming pattern in a lusty, the-more-the-merrier manner. Some ministers eat out their frustrations at the dinner table, not so much to be merry as to assuage hostility. Others become finicky to the point of fanaticism. This is an unfailing method of gaining attention. Food for some stills the gnawing awareness of failure—that burning sensation in the pit of the stomach. The presence of these complications makes the matter of proper eating habits complex and involved. A wife can be an expert nutritionist and yet fail to keep her husband healthy. Many times she has to be aware of deeper problems than calories, vitamins, and the inevitable yellow vegetable.

There is an unhealthy preoccupation with food in this country. Eating and refraining from eating enjoy widespread and unwarranted attention. We are a diet-crazed people. This may be due in part to a fundamental embarrassment over our plenty in the midst of such great want. It would be sad if the minister and his family merely added to this preoccupation with food. If dieting becomes his lot, the minister should confine himself to silence as much as is feasible.

It is strange how little genuine satisfaction is gained in our consumption of such wonderful rich and varied food. We often eat so rapidly and under so much strain that we are scarcely aware of flavor, aroma, and other subtleties of food. There is a movie of Tibetan monks partaking of their evening meal. It shows the men crouched around a large bowl. Each man has a small bowl for his own portion. Each man is consuming with gusto. The narrator informs the audience that the food consists of a tasteless gruel, and that the menu is always the same. Why the obvious enjoyment of such food? Perhaps because they consider the food a direct gift from God, plus the fact of their relaxed attitude during the meal. We too need to learn how to relax and enjoy our meals.

Some weeks a minister may find that meal time is his only family time. It is important that time is spent by the wife in offering an attractive table for this family time. There will always be the spilt milk and the sticky crumbs while the children are young, yet these can remain a minor theme rather than the major setting of a meal.

It is necessary for a pastor's wife to spend more money for food than she would like. This is to enable her to serve fresh fruits and vegetables, and lean meats, rather than starchy foods. The meals which the husband consumes away from home are frequently heavy. The day scheduled for a man's luncheon downtown may suggest a light fruit salad at dinner time. A wise physician suggested to a clergyman that he eat only half a hotel or restaurant serving of each item except meat. As the years accumulate, so does weight. A minister may want to eliminate bread and dessert from his away-from-home menu.

Modern clergy are rediscovering the values of fasting. Fasting may be done under the direction of a physician without endangering the health. The benefits in spiritual rewards have long been known by religious persons.

There is a great wealth of information available on diet. No one who is literate need go ignorant on this subject. The gaining of knowledge of the subject, plus a determined program of action based upon that knowledge, should result in a healthy husband. Good stewardship involves the care of the body to the best of our ability. The abuse of the body by neglect or overindulgence is a sign of unfaithfulness to an instrument of God.

Once a parson is well pruned, his wife may want to turn her attention to his grooming. Men are not always amenable to good grooming. They have a tendency to feel that when they have on trousers and a coat it is done. This is a direct result of dullness in the male wardrobe. Yet this very dullness and conservatism in male attire makes it possible for the minister to be as well dressed as the next fellow.

Before a young wife gets too involved in improving her husband's appearance, she should be warned that some men defy improvement. There is a type of male who always looks crumpled. This male wrinkles a wrinkleproof suit and wilts a wiltproof collar. He never looks shaved, and his hair never stays combed. Baldness is an improvement for these men, but they are usually the type who scarcely lose a hair. Wifely treatment in these cases is frustrating.

Most men can improve their appearance with a wife's co-operation. Some men manage to be neat in spite of a wife who is more hindrance than help. Usually a husband's appearance reflects a wife's habit patterns. A man who must dwell in a messy house is apt to appear unkempt in public. Ministers cannot afford bad grooming. They must at least make the effort to appear fresh and neat at all times.

Cleanliness is the basic ingredient of grooming. The daily bath habit is a double blessing, for it also provides a man with a time to relax and cogitate. He has time to be alone with his thoughts. Well manicured nails, a clean shave, and frequent haircuts give a man a lift as well as improve the impression he makes on others.

The popularity of conservative colors in clothing for all men has increased the availability of clothes for ministers. Good quality clothing is always a good investment, especially in the important wardrobe items. A minister ought to avoid buying his suits at Jake's Place off the plain lead-pipe rack—that is, unless he is something of a connoisseur in these matters. Usually he needs the best advice he can get as to fit and style.

His work shirts are white. There is no part of a man's wardrobe which can so quickly make him look unkempt as his white collar. The immaculate white collar not only enhances a man's appearance but it also sustains the tired ego. Unless a wife is something of a specialist in ironing, the shirt belongs to the professional laundry. This is a sound investment both from the standpoint of good grooming and as a safeguard to happy domestic relations. Nothing can be more upsetting to a minister's household than to have no white shirt available. It is much easier on the marriage if the laundry can be blamed and not the telltale baskets or unironed shirts.

When a professional laundering service is used it is just as well to purchase medium priced shirts. The more expensive shirts look and feel just a little bit better, but that is hardly worth the extra expense as the shirts wear out at a steady rate regardless of the quality. It is much better to have a larger number of shirts of lesser quality so that the cupboard need never be bare. There must be at least one clean white shirt per day. This is not the place to scrimp and save on laundry. Many days will require two shirt changes.

It is becoming increasingly difficult to tell a minister from other men in a group. This is considered a step in the right direction by most clergy, yet it leads to some interesting situations. One minister moved into a new neighborhood. During the period when the neighbors were conjecturing about who the new people were, and what the husband did for a living, one woman was absolutely certain he must be a bartender. The hours he kept had convinced her of this. This sort of thing could be avoided by the simple addition of a clerical collar!

For the neophyte clergyman emerging from his crew-cut casual college days, the purchase of the first hat may be a traumatic experience. A man needs love and tender care as he views himself for the first time in a hat. Male headgear is so ridiculous every man looks strange and disoriented in his first hat. A wife needs uncommon maturity to refrain from screaming at the sight. As age takes its toll, the hat is worn with less self-consciousness and even a touch of confidence. It is also discovered to be a way of keeping an increasingly barren scalp warm.

Ties are an inevitable means of self-expression simply because they are the only creative outlet a man has in his dress. Ministers have a special attraction to red ties, which may or may not have some hidden significance. A variety of colors might help spice up life a bit.

Whatever else might be said about a minister's wardrobe, it must require minimum attention from him. This means a lot of attention and work for his wife. She must stock the drawers and tend the closet. One wife never could make the transition from the clothesline to the drawer on schedule. That is, until the day her husband appeared at the top of the stairs clad in his altogether and bellowed for his shorts. This was the usual procedure for Tuesday. Except this Tuesday one of the ladies of the church was standing in the doorway at the foot of the stairs. Lessons should be learned at less cost in embarrassment.

Handkerchiefs can also be a source of embarrassment. One minister developed a phobia about handkerchiefs after he had pulled his carefully folded kerchief from his pocket to wipe his hardworking brow during a sermon. Its careful folds concealed an enormous hole. His wife thereafter developed a pattern of folds: oblong folds were safe to open in public, square folds meant danger.

Good grooming is a basic ingredient in self-confidence. It is therefore worthy of attention. Grooming is facilitated by routine. Once a young man develops a pattern of self-care he saves himself the necessity of deciding each morning whether he will bathe, or shave, or perform the other jobs involved in grooming. In the contemporary setting in which most ministers are doing their work, it seems a justifiable effort to achieve the well-groomed appearance.

9

*how to unbend
without falling on your face*

Strange occurrences sometimes bring a wife to understand her husband's needs. A minister and his family were camping in the Rockies. The father and his sons discovered the joys of floating down the rushing mountain stream on the air mattresses. This was long before the use of air mattresses in water was considered fashionable, or even normal behavior. The wife was delightedly watching the fun from the bank when she noticed she was not alone. A little old lady was at her side, wringing her hands with anxiety. Suddenly she turned to the minister's wife and said, "Is that your husband?" This relationship established, she said forebodingly, "You should let him out more often."

Ministers do need to be let out more often. And their wives right along with them. Ministers and their wives are always going somewhere, but seldom can it be described as "out." This "out" is getting away from parishioners and church concerns just for fun.

There is a natural tendency to want to just stay home if such a thing as a free evening occurs. It is important to stay home and relax with the family as frequently as possible. Yet staying home does not provide the same ingredients of fun as going out does. Ministers have a tendency to keep aware of church work all the time they are at home. It takes effort to win complete distraction.

Ministers need to get out more often because they take themselves too seriously. Observing many clergy at close range, one gets the impression that if they relaxed, they might fall apart. It is perfectly logical for a minister to take himself seriously: the job is serious, the people he works with are often desperate, the consequences of his action can be deadly serious. It is because it is so serious a business that relaxation becomes so vital.

People say that having a good time is a simple matter. All it takes is time and money. This is a snare and a delusion. The ability to engage in genuine fun is a rare and precious thing. It cannot be bought with any amount of money, although it can be facilitated by it. Freedom from work restraints does not assure leisure-time fun. Leisure can be a strain and a bore.

Fun is almost as illusive to capture as is love. It is not the kind of commodity which one possesses and hangs onto. It is as difficult to wish into being as is love. Our constitutional right to pursue happiness deludes us into thinking it is an entity in itself. It is, of course, the by-product of the good life.

When one contemplates the lives of saints, one is amazed at the exuberant joy apparent in their living. On the other hand, what is more miserable than the individual devoted to pursuing good times? We confuse fun with the frantic pursual of an erotic assortment of titillating experiences. This may be escape, but it isn't necessarily fun. There is value in escape, but it ought to be a rewarding rather than a punitive experience. The fruits of our relaxation ought to be manifest in more rewarding work.

It is important for a minister to learn the art of leisure. To use leisure creatively is a common problem of all men and as such deserves his attention. But use of leisure must not become a humanitarian problem to be solved.

What is going out, having fun, enjoying leisure, and getting relaxation? It is many things, and different things to various kinds of people. It is certainly to be defined as something everyone wants, needs, and pursues to some degree. We are supplied and encouraged on all hands with equipment for its pursual. Yet one can gather up all the traditional ingredients for a good time, in lavish quantity, and end up being miserable.

For example, a group of ministers and their wives had been meeting in a serious fashion for two years. They presented papers in turn on subjects of vital interest to one another. As one year came to a close, someone suggested a party just for fun. This group of people had all the ingredients necessary to a bang-up party. Almost every one of them had led successful parties for others. There was talent of all kinds available within the group.

They all knew how to help others have a good time. But the party was a miserable failure. It was comparable to a couple of joke-book compilers trying to amuse each other with stories. And about that successful. They were all self-conscious and the evening was stilted and a bore.

In an informal post-mortem of that occasion, some ministers commented that the serious meetings had been more fun. The goodnights in front of half-held open doors were highlights of conviviality. Perhaps there is something to be learned from this experience. That is, that fun may have to flow from meaningful experience for the more intellectualized individual. Trying to manufacture fun is a dreary business for the thoughtful person.

It happens that fun is to be found in the pursuance of the daily work. Doing the hard job with the light touch can bring genuine enjoyment. Yet this kind of fun is not enough. There must be an alternation from the work and thought pattern of the daily round of activity.

The way to have fun for each individual has to be found. Just because George has fun playing golf, don't assume John will also. The frantic search for good times tends to follow a pattern. The whole country seems to go on one kind of kick after another. To follow the trend does not assure amusement.

Many ministers shun fun because they believe it costs money. Going out to dine may cost more than eating the meal at home. Yet one is making an investment in a commodity which enriches life— recreative relaxation. There are many free ways to go out for there are museums to see, communities to investigate in the surrounding areas, and nature to enjoy. However, it is a good discipline for a serious person to spend money for good times.

Occasional outings do not relax the way regularly planned occasions do. Time to relax is the most urgent when the schedule is the most heavy. This is why the old Hollywood idea that husbands take out wives does not apply in the parsonage. A minister's wife must take it upon herself to plan and insist on recreation. Recreation must not be left to the time when there is nothing left to do. There is no such time in the life of a minister.

Planned recreation becomes a pleasant reality when a minister has first learned how to relax some time each day. Living under constant tension takes too great a toll. A wife should help her husband feel the importance of relaxation. Many ministers can't sit down to read without feeling guilty, or they find a nap before dinner impossible for the same reason. Some men have to endure a heart attack before the message gets to them that relaxation is part of the work. Ministers hear so often the snide remarks about working only on Sunday they are overly conscientious about time. It is understandable that they do not want the layman to be encouraged in this outrageous idea about the ministry.

It helps immeasureably if a minister can come home to a relaxed household. A wife has to learn loving acceptance of her husband's relaxation. This is as important to its fulfillment as any other single factor. Even when she cannot get out the back door because the snow hasn't been shoveled, or the dog reeks for want of a bath, or it's July and the screens aren't on, she must resist the temptation to interfere with relaxation when it is desperately needed.

Individuals vary greatly in the amount of pressure they can bear. Most are subject to the same danger signals. One sure sign of strain is overreaction to stimuli. If a man angers too quickly, laughs nervously, or cannot control his emotions while preaching, he is in danger of emotional explosion. Simple relaxation may not cure these problems, but it will help. Preoccupation to the point of ignoring wife and family can also be a sign of stress. One minister, when he at last took his wife to a movie, slept soundly through the picture. Work without relaxation becomes a treadmill and looses its satisfaction. Tasks become overly difficult when one is too exhausted to perform them. Exhaustion has a way of accumulating in the ministry. A night's sleep doesn't always give enough strength for the ensuing day. There must be time for relaxation during each work day.

Sometimes props are needed to slow down a tense man. A hobby may furnish this necessary distraction of attention from his job. If one believed everything one read, one would come to the conclusion that it is dangerous not to have a hobby. This is an overstatement of the hobby case, for many perfectly normal individuals have survived with distinction without a single hobby. Hobbies have a way of getting out of hand. They multiply at about the speed of rabbits. Some highly geared men ride the hobby as tensely as they work on the job. The hobby for them becomes another task to be finished no matter what. A hobby needs one basic requirement: whatever it is it can be laid aside until it molds, rusts, evaporates, or perhaps, all three. If a hobby isn't a take-it-or-leave-it proposition, it isn't a hobby.

For ministers there is a pre-test before a hobby

can be pursued. It is an aptitude test for doing nothing with ease and enjoyment. Once he masters the art of loafing, then he is ready to tackle a hobby. Ministers tend to become addicted to activity. It is tragic if their leisure is simply an extension of activity for its own sake.

Learning to unbend is not an option but a necessity for a minister. Churches with foresight recognize this and insist that the minister have a day off. Many men find themselves so exhausted by the time this day of the week comes, they are physically and emotionally unable to plan any activity for it. A wife may have to learn to plan. She can begin by keeping her own schedule free of meetings on that day. She may want to suggest short trips or things to do away from the house for part of the day. Most of all, she must learn not to push. Her minister might just fall on his face!

10

Saturday night always comes before Sunday morning

While Saturday night is for howling among the general populace, for the minister it is a night of quiet preparation. A few clergy feel that they too can howl on Saturdays and successfully do so. For most men, Saturday tends to have an aura of tension and near crisis. As tension rises, a sensitive wife learns the art of being seen and not heard. A man in the throes of sermon preparation is easily distracted and has a low threshold of irritability.

The continued acceptance of the sermon in our culture is something of a phenomenon. When one considers the constant barrage of written and spoken words endured by modern man, one wonders with surprise about the large number of people who submit themselves Sunday after Sunday to the words of a preacher. What is more, it is difficult to switch off a sermon in mid-point. Yet the same people who listen through the sermon may have turned off the President in the course of his speech just the night before. The people enjoy much perogative in the matter of what they will and will not hear. The sermon deserves to be taken seriously, therefore, and ought to receive first-class attention and labor.

When a wife assents to this priority of the sermon, she immediately fashions her behavior in such a way as to convey to the husband her respect for his efforts in its completion. This can bolster a minister's own realization of the importance of the sermon as nothing else can.

Even if the sermon is completed early in the week, perhaps at the church office, Saturday night is still a time of preparation for Sunday-morning worship. The best way to prepare for worship will vary with individuals. Preparation often runs the gamut between a day off for play to a day spent in quiet, prayerful retreat. Whatever the decision is about Saturday night, the results should serve Sunday in the best possible manner. Sunday should find the minister at his freshest, not the left-over tatters of a hectic night out. Many ministers have made it a rule of their life never to stay out after ten o'clock on Saturday.

Some wives have the urge to help their husband write his sermon. Sermon preparation is not a group project; it is the outpouring from the heart of an individual. A politician can afford to have his speeches ghosted, but it is a sad day when a preacher resorts to such tactics.

Is there a function for the wife in relation to the sermon other than keeping her hands off? There is the crucial area of her reaction to the preached and finished product. A lifetime could be spent by a wife in learning how to best respond to the sermon. Whatever she may decide upon, she must remember that sermonizing is always an extending of the ego. This is true in its best and in its crudest sense. As sensitive as a man is about his ego, he will also be about his preaching.

Early in marriage, one wife proceeded on the theory that all her husband's sermons were peerless examples of oratorical and theological perfection. She said so with conviction. After what she hopefully described as her maturing, she felt the necessity of giving some constructive criticism. She decided to be absolutely honest in conveying her own reactions to each sermon. When her minister laid an egg large enough to be carried by two, she helped him carry it—honest faced and light hearted. Then she took a course in psychology for ministers' wives.

This course was built around an uncompromising premise: never give negative criticism. She was taught that negative criticism only helps the criticized know why he loathes the criticizer. She was scared nearly to death. Fortunately for her her husband had been strong enough to survive her onslaughts.

A sensitive minister may come to the point where he realizes that it is an unfair burden upon a wife to always comment upon the sermon. He may realize this intellectually but emotionally he still yearns for her supporting words. If a wife comments upon the sermon only at those times when she has a positive and helpful word to say perhaps her opinion will be more highly regarded.

The experts are most confusing and contradictory. Some advise a wife to always praise, even if the praise is confined to the diction. Yet praise for the sake of praise can become an insult to the man of integrity. Others insist that the minister's wife owes it to her husband to be honest and to help him improve his sermon effort. This approach is to dare before angels. One's motivation in finding fault must be pure as the driven snow. It is too facile to allow the sermon to become the whipping boy of a wife's frustration.

Not many ministers are Fosdicks and Tittles. These giants of the faith probably had their bad days. Is it then too much to expect the average minister to avoid failure in the pulpit? The layman expects the minister to always be amenable to criticism of the sermon. Very few ministers suffer from a lack of critical appraisal from the congregation. With this abundance in mind, a wife might wisely confine herself to rare well-timed efforts at constructive criticism. The less able a man is in preaching, the less he needs to be criticized. The able man may be lulled by a constant flow of praise; he could profit from an occasional barb.

Sermonizing has changed a great deal in recent years. The jolly optimism of the twenties and thirties, expressed itself in the anecdotal sermon.

While the sermons were idealistic, many had an almost flippant quality. This had apparently replaced the more classical, orotund mode of earlier preaching. The current mood of the theological world is serious and sober. Many young preachers emerging from today's seminaries are intense and quite devoid of humor in their sermons. They are hard on the listener. Without diminishing the seriousness of their message, many ministers can add some relief from the relentless onslaught of hard truth.

Some preachers belittle the importance of the sermon. When they do, it is usually to rationalize their own inadequacy or desire to dig in and produce worthy material. A wife must never allow herself to underestimate the importance of the sermon. She must always maintain an attitude of expectancy toward the coming sermon, as well as appreciation for the one past.

There is no point in a man's ministry so difficult for him to evaluate. The excellent preacher is frequently the least sure of himself. He may be constantly castigating himself for unreal failures. A mediocre man tends to plug along at an uneven pace without very strong feeling about success or failure. The man who is incapable of doing a creditable job is usually aware of his drawback to some extent. However, he may be tempted to twist his inner sense of evaluation to the point where he seems to be confident of himself. The wife of the man who simply cannot preach must endure with courage and love her husband's inadequacy. She will suffer very much because such a failure is hard to conceal unless she can help her husband to express his talents in a wider, more specialized ministry. It is fortunate that the ministry is so wide in its area of concern a man can shine in one aspect with great enough illumination to shadow his failure in another.

Ministers sometimes have a favorite horse to ride, or axe to grind. It is hard to be equally interested in everything. It is also difficult for a man to keep his preaching topics various and inclusive. It is quite possible to change the topic without changing the actual content of a sermon. One minister was quite famous for being able to use the texts of the church year and still confine himself to two subjects. No matter the text, he could apply it in but two ways. A wife might be brave enough to suggest ways of varying the content of sermons.

A wife can encourage her husband to be forthright in his preaching. Sermons have a tendency to fall into two broad categories—they shock or soothe. The soothing variety sometimes bore but are usually the kind the layman enjoys. Wives have a tendency to be very brave at home while encouraging their husbands on to some positive stand. The bravery frequently turns to cowardice as she sits elbow to elbow listening to the sermon with the congregation. She does not have the comfort of a pulpit to hide behind. She can feel the tenseness of the listeners around her. This is understandable for many times a wife will feel the repercussions in a congregation before her husband will. She may feel that life is complicated enough without having her husband stir up a hornet's nest in his sermon. But the gospel preached forthrightly is not always soothing. More frequently the gospel must both shock and soothe. The more timely the message of the gospel is made, the more dangerous it becomes. If a husband's preaching is always praised and is always soothing, he may be in danger of preaching something other than the gospel.

When we look with objectivity and see how little change in behavior results from most preaching, we know we must always be brave. The conundrum of our time is the popularity of church attendance concurrent with the popularity of sin on all levels of society. The sword of Christ is two-edged. When a minister preaches the whole gospel, he is often bruised. His wife suffers with him.

Preaching the word in this century is as dangerous as it ever was. It is easier to be brave when a wife thinks less of what Mrs. Gotrocks thinks of the sermon and more of what God thinks of it.

It is a great tragedy that a minister and his wife seldom hear other men preach. The few opportunities which come during vacations ought to be cherished. Guest preachers invited to share the pulpit will also be a blessing. Wives have to encourage their husbands to listen to other men. Clergymen have a tendency to be poor listeners. They are fidgety and preoccupied as an audience. Many become bored to death with hearing anyone's voice but their own. This is a tragic situation. Ministers need very much to listen to their brothers both as a method of learning more, and as a way of self-discipline.

It may sound somewhat strange to suggest that how one gets ready for church influences the worship service. Most ministers and their wives endure hectic weeks. Sunday morning can be the last straw. What is more, one can look like the last rose. Hair that was shampooed earlier in the week, and dresses that were worn to important weekday occasions, appear on Sunday as haggard and disarrayed. This kind of appearance is unworthy the occasion. The corporate experience of worship is the greatest event of our lives. It deserves only our best. When worship takes its rightful place in the pattern of our lives, all other occasions of life fall into proper relationship.

A young wife may be embarrassed when a parishioner comments on the sermon. One newly-wed was so unhinged by a layman's remark about her husband's sermon, she said: "Oh, it really wasn't anything." The more experienced wife may learn to say: "I thought it was wonderful too. But, of course, I always think so, I'm so prejudiced."

11

the ego and you

A Sunday menu including roast parson is enjoyed by many. The sermon is the focal point of these discussions, but the criticism or praise is not confined to the sermonizing. It is always open season on ministers. Everybody qualifies as an expert on clergymen. There is one bright spot: a minister is seldom ignored.

Because this is so, a minister's ego needs special attention. The term "ego" is frequently thought to be negative, as though it were something to be rid of. Yet the ego has a vital function in the fulfillment of personality. In any event, the ego cannot be eliminated; it must be endured. It is good for a minister's wife to understand some of the strain under which a pastor's ego must exist. A minister's ego is battered constantly from all sides in innumerable ways.

Laymen tend to divide into three categories in relation to the minister's ego. The bulk of the members of a church are fairly level-headed about each minister. They praise and criticize in appropriate, if not equal, portions. According to the law of averages they tend to cancel out one another. The ego suffers not overly much in their hands. It remains for the other two categories to do most of the damage. One group consists of persons who believe the minister is incapable of doing anything right. If he does, it is surely a mistake. The other group believes he can do no wrong.

It is as difficult for the ego to accept a constant barrage of commendation as it is of condemnation, although the former is easier to take. Those who fawn over your husband rarely do him any lasting good. They offer a momentary illusion of being sustained through some windy blast of criticism, but a minister of insight knows this is not the genuine thing. The kind word at the right moment from a solid citizen is what a minister needs in the crisis. Nothing is quite so effective as the reassuring word from the former critic.

A minister needs a hide like an elephant, yet he cannot afford the luxury of an insensitive skin. He needs both criticism and praise, just as surely as he needs food and water. Almost all ministers suffer indignities at the hand of unscrupulous individuals. It is usually those least qualified to make criticism who are freest to offer it.

There is a strange aspect of criticism which is difficult to comprehend. A minister may be all but smothered in a heavy blanket of love by his congregation, yet one small word of criticism will be a crushing experience. An unkind word can literally undo weeks and months, sometimes years, of solid work. It can leave an otherwise normal man in a state of indecision about himself and his work. The unkind criticism outweighs a barrel of kind words.

Criticism is a fact of life for ministers, their wives, their children and their dogs. If one tries with diligence, one can understand intellectually why this is so. Whether the heart will understand is another matter.

The church is the one place where all are welcomed. It is perhaps the one organization in the world which seeks everyone as a member in good standing. The minister is not able to pick and choose his members. The church seeks out especially the lost, the lonely, the disenchanted, the disenfranchised, the rejected, the unlovable, the irascible, the indifferent and even the cruel. Is it any wonder such persons have become part of the fellowship? The church will always be a mixture of the difficult and the dear. The church is to redeem and transform the difficult, and that is precisely the process in which we are so involved.

The church is the one public place in the world where one can vent one's gall, relieve one's frustrations, reveal one's distortions, and still expect to be heard. The church, representing her Christ, does not strike back, but absorbs hostility and abuse. The minister and his family are the logical targets of much of this hostility. It is one of the ways to suffer for his sake, yet it seems so undramatic and humiliating. When we try to understand the motivation behind much of the lashing out at the minister, we realize it is not so much the individual who is attacked as the truth which he represents. This is true no matter how personal the form of the attack may be. A minister often personifies

to the hostile individual the demands of disciple-
ship which that person intends to reject. Criticism
becomes a shield against the penetrating light of
the gospel.

It is very difficult to tell this irrational critic
from the person who is trying to offer constructive
criticism. Frequently the two elements are inter-
twined. A minister can make use of good criticism
tendered in love, he cannot afford to dismiss all
criticism as irrational. Yet no matter how constructive criticism may be, it is hard to receive.
Ministers set up all kinds of barriers against receiving criticism. Some become all things to all men.
At the other extreme are men who purposely in-
cite criticism. Everything they do asks for it. They
are constantly reiterating to everyone how much
they are going through. This is a pitiful kind of
self-martyrdom, and well deserved. It is self-
inflicted by way of other persons.

To avoid these awful extremes should be the
goal of every clergyman. Many years of enduring
criticism sometimes produces cynicism and bitterness about people. The bitterness sometimes ex-
presses itself in attacks on the laity or upon the
hierarchy of the church. Cynicism must have no
place in the life of a minister.

Most ministers eventually learn to take criticism in moderate good humor. Praise is another matter, and is often taken far too seriously. It can only be taken seriously when it is essentially praise for God, as seen through a particular servant of his. Some excellent ministers have been sacrificed on the altar of praise. Too much praise has caused them to halt their growth and stagnate in a pool of self-satisfaction. There was a famous clergyman of obvious stature who inspired many audiences throughout the country twenty years ago. He is delivering essentially the identical speech today. He scarcely needs to be conscious to deliver it any more. This is a disaster. The speech itself is excellent, audiences may still profit by it. Yet one is certain that the man has lost his vitality and his desire to grow.

An essential element in any individual's reaction to praise is a sense of unworthiness. It is apropos to remember Jesus' admonition to the man who called him "good."

It would be misleading if what is said here gives the impression that the ego is easily disciplined by the proper rules. Nothing would be further from the fact. All efforts to the contrary, a minister's ego can get him in a great deal of trouble. Some men have allowed their egos to ruin their ministry, their health, and even their homes. There are those who find it impossible to refuse a request to speak. Tangled schedules are the result. Other ministers have subtle ways of constantly being at the center of every group in the church. There was a church where no meeting dared begin without the minister's presence. This proved an efficient and most thorough method of eliminating lay leadership.

Then there is the minister of the reversed ego. He insists in many ways that he is more humble than anyone. His steady diet of humble pie is a neat cover up for an inflated sense of importance. As devious as the ways of all men are, so are the ways of ministers. The problem comes where the minister's ego interferes with the effectiveness of his lifework.

In proportion as a husband's ego suffers, a wife will suffer also. Sometimes the results come in direct assault upon the marriage. Usually a wife feels her husband's suffering by the indirect means of empathetic understanding. There is not much a wife can do to lessen the occasional blows a minister does suffer. Perhaps the best she can offer is her total love. Occasionally she may inject some objectivity in a situation by keeping her own composure when her husband may be under fire.

There is really only one way for a minister to deal with his ego. Every day of his life he must surrender it to God. At the onset, and at the weary conclusion, of each day, he must be able to say, "Nevertheless, not my will, but thine, be done."

12

ambition: help or hindrance?

Any innocent bystander on the American road of life is aware of the tremendous role played by ambition. Ours is a culture filled to overflowing with clichés about success. Every little boy is imbued with these ideas of getting on in the world. He is

taught by precept and example that the more ambition one has the better. But should this little boy
decide to enter the ministry, he will soon discover
that here is the profession in life which proves the
rule by being the exception.

Almost everyone agrees that any show of ambition in a minister is unbecoming, uncouth, and un-
fortunate. It would be to every minister's advantage if he could eliminate this aspect of his
early training. However, ambition is not easily
exorcised. Once introduced into one's life pattern
at a tender age it is difficult if not almost impossible to delete. And there also remains a per-
sistently annoying question, "Can one really get
along without ambition?" Upon consideration it
seems evident that a man devoid of ambition either
for himself or others is rather a dull one. If a person is not interested in going any place, he is
likely to be quite a bore where he is.

Yet so many ministers suffer severely a sense of
guilt about ambitious thoughts. They feel they
are not being loyal to their deepest convictions.
The desire for success in the ministry becomes a
painful experience, and often the fulfillment of
the dream is itself bitter brew. The successful minister always feels some estrangement from those

who are left behind. This is true in most professions, but it is twice true in the ministry.

There are all kinds and sorts of ambition. One appropriate and essential kind is what Paul called "ambition for Christ." We are not concerned with the implications of this sort of ambition in this chapter. This is a part of a man's basic motivation for entering the ministry. We are rather concerned with the more earthy desire to get ahead in whatever the field of endeavor. It is pure silliness to assume that ministers are not going to want to achieve in this more mundane manner.

The fact is the ministry is filled with very ambitious men. If it were not so, the church would surely be in the doldrums. The ministry is filled with men of extraordinary leadership ability, filled with creative ideas, and motivated at the deepest level by Christian convictions. They are aware of the direction of their own lives and of the lives of others. This is part of the reason it is such an exciting and wonderful thing to have the care and feeding of such men.

The problem comes at the point where the ambition is expressed. For the greatest number of men the desire for success in their work is kept within the limits of the immediate work at hand.

All, or almost all, of their ambition can be consumed in the day-to-day tasks.

There are a few sorts who wear their ambition full face forward. If this ambition is tempered with a large dose of conviviality they are apt to get by very well in the church world. Their less obnoxious attempts to get ahead of everyone else will be taken with good humor. Somehow one can manage to tolerate the man who is honest about his desire to be on the top, especially so if that desire is tempered by a real concern for those he leaves behind.

There is an even smaller number of men who are just plain ambitious but who have not the good grace to own up to it. They gain high places by maneuvering and usually at great cost to others. If they are clever men, they can fool a lot of the people most of the time. It is comforting to know they cannot fool Him.

Some very ambitious men do not realize this force for what it is. They seem quite unaware that they suffer from unfulfilled desires and they are apt to confuse their unhappiness with other aspects of their lives. Many wives become the target of this discontent. His ambition is what is ailing him, but since she is easier to see, he blames her.

The trouble with ambition is that it tends to be out of proportion to one's ability to realize it.

Often the person with very little gift will be possessed of a monstrous ambition. The frustration which results is monumental.

When a man is frustrated of his ambition, he may pervert his desire to get ahead in such a way as to seek more failure. In an effort to deny himself his ambition which he cannot achieve, he may punish himself by repeated humiliations which would otherwise be avoided. This is evident in the man who feels his fellow ministers look down on him. He begins to withdraw from contact with them, and begins to refuse leadership among them when it is offered. This can result only in great tragedy.

This is to say that ambition is not a thing to be taken lightly and dismissed from serious consideration. Its presence has to be recognized. Just to realize the presence of ambition in an open and unashamed way is half the battle won. But what shall one do with it? How can it be a help rather than a hindrance in the ministry?

Quite obviously ambition must be kept under controls. It may cause a man to jump from one job into another at every offer. He may feel he cannot refuse a change because it is a promotion. Many times he will be on the very verge of some important and crucial achievement in his present parish, yet he cannot resist another call. This is one expression of ambition which has to be controlled.

For some, politicking is the outlet for ambition. Church politicking can be done ever so politely. It can be simply a matter of keeping one's name in obvious places, or getting to be known by the right persons in the right places. This type of man is a great attender. He has even been known to offer his services as a speaker.

Whatever the controls necessary for the individual man must be determined by himself. No man can be content to stand first on one foot and then on the other. Every man must from time to time move forward, at least one foot in front of the other. And occasionally a man needs to take that giant step. The discontent with standing in one place can be a holy one. It is certainly unthinkable for the average man to serve the same church of limited membership all his days. A man can hardly serve a church of a hundred members which quite surely taxed his best imagination during seminary when he is forty. Active and creative men have to move ahead into large situations. As the older men retire from the positions of high leadership in the church, younger men must be ready and able, as well as willing to take over their responsibilities.

Every man must from time to time come to grips with his future. How a man deals with his future is of great concern to any wife who cares. She has to understand the forces which motivate him, or which restrain him.

The future is always an intriguing and illusive part of life. For reasons beyond understanding for most of us, the future, which is not yet, can profoundly affect the present which now is. A future which does not really exist can still torture and twist a man in his present which does exist. The tragedy inherent in this Penelope's web is that living can almost be halted in the present while one lives projected into a dream-induced future. It is so very easy once one begins to look into the possible future prospects to forget to live where one is.

It is possible for all of us to get caught in this delusion of the future prospect primarily because there is in all of our lives enough heartache and discomfort and/or ennui where we are to make any other possibility rosy. The result of becoming enmeshed in a pattern of future hope is that we become disillusioned with our present again and again. We begin to think of the present as merely a stepping-stone to the future. When the job at hand becomes merely a way-station on the way to the Big Job then it can hardly command our full and undivided attention.

Yet there are times in almost every minister's life when he feels his present situation has lost its challenge, if not its charm, for him. This is not a figment of the imagination; many times it is a reflection of the facts. All men feel the need to be stretched to their maximum, to be able to give all they want to give, to produce to the limits of their abilities. They also feel a desperate need to have what they offer received by those to whom it is proffered. Sometimes due to circumstances beyond the control of the minister himself, the situation begins to close to him. At such times as this, a minister and his wife must look into their future.

Perhaps to say "all men need to be stretched" is too inclusive a statement. There is always present and real danger of living on past achievement. This can happen at an alarmingly tender age. Some men barely into their thirties begin each sentence with, "When I was at Podunk Center. . . ." It is so nice and comfortable to have past achievements. They are there to be looked back upon occasionally when the spirit moves us, but dwelling in the storehouse of the past can be a suffocating experience.

Failure as well as success spurs ambition. The heartbreak of failure makes a man want to be somewhere else. The rationalizations of failure are filled with "theys." It can take years to fill in the "me." If only one could get the right church in the right town at the right time! This may very well be the answer. There are parishes where anything but failure is inconceivable. There is evil entrenched in high places in some communities where resistance to the gospel is staggering. Men are daily sacrificed to these parishes. "They" are sometimes the cause of a minister's failure.

No man should have to deal with failure by himself. Beyond his God, he needs the understanding of another human. However much another person might want to help alleviate the suffering of failure, yet the great burden of it must be borne by the person who has failed. A wife can help with the healing of hurts. The immature wife may find herself wanting to strike out at "they." She may be tempted to speak out in her husband's defense. This is seldom effective and occasionally disastrous. Strangely enough, some wives find themselves striking out at the husband. It is sometimes a temptation for an intelligent and gifted wife to berate her husband in his failure. She is always eager to improve upon his ministry, correct his mistakes, and make him a better man. While her motivation may be admirable, no man is able to bear such treatment for long. He will either resent her, or treat her more desperately than that.

The Horatio problem is not all in the minister. Many wives burn with ambition for their husbands. The problem is accentuated to an impossible degree if the wife is actually more gifted and highly motivated than her spouse. Some women just push and push and push because in their own self-confidence they simply cannot conceive the lack of such sureness on the part of their mate.

While the problems of relating to a husband who may be failing are admittedly great, yet there can be tremendous satisfactions for the wife who is a genuine help during these periods. Occasionally a time of failure is in fact a time of triumph. It may also prove a time of coming together of great preciousness between husband and wife. The hurts of life often teach us how much we are dependent upon one another.

Good times, success, brief triumphs, come to every man in the ministry. Perhaps less often than one might wish, but they are there. It may well be that to care for the man who is very successful is the most difficult task of all. Time, energy, and attention, come at a premium when a man is in great demand. The wife of the successful man must learn self-sufficiency which minimizes her demands.

They must be of such a nature that they can be borne with delight by her husband.

Ambition which is constantly thwarted and submerged has a tendency to break loose on occasion and cause us considerable embarassment. One of the nice things about ambition is that it can be diverted to good ends before it becomes a problem. We can learn to use our own desires for success on behalf of others. We can be ambitious for our friends, our enemies, and find tremendous satisfaction in this way.

The ability to be joyous in a deep and satisfying manner when a friend has a triumph in the ministry is a great grace. Very few people seem to be able to really enjoy another man's good fortune— especially if it is in his same field of endeavor. A few people seem to be gifted quite naturally with the ability to be sincerely happy over another's success. To be ambitious for others is one outlet for the craving for success in one's own life.

The relationship of the sense of call to promotion and change of parish has been quite deliberately avoided by this mere woman. This is a subject which defies analysis by any amateur. A few questions do occasionally plague a thinking woman: Why are calls always to bigger situations? Or almost always? Why does more than one man feel the same call at the same time to the same church? And so on and on one might ask pertinent questions. The answers are probably not available to the average minister. It remains his lot to sincerely evaluate his own inner convictions against the best advice of his contemporaries. If his ambition does not get out of hand he will always find himself in the right place at the right time. That is, wherever we are is in the deepest sense God-chosen. We are to live in the moment and place with confidence, preferably that "lively confidence" defined by Martin Luther.

13

the best has been saved
for the last

Much has been said here on the care and feeding of ministers which might frighten a young wife. The best news is that a wife may fail to live up to expectations in any and all of the areas mentioned and yet be an excellent minister's wife. For a minister can afford to sacrifice all secondary attributes of a good wife if she is a loving and loyal helpmate. Love and loyalty alone do endure as the foundation of a happy home. A loving wife is better than a bushel of good conduct medals.

A minister seems to need more love and affection than most men. This may be because he is constantly drained of his own resources by the demands of others. He depends upon his marriage for renewal and stability, and as a place where he may refresh himself. It is therefore of utmost urgency that his marriage is given thoughtful attention and depth of understanding.

It is to the advantage of a minister to be thoroughly married. To be thoroughly married is a rare and precious thing in our time. Marriage has suffered severe blows since the early 1900's. Just at the moment when women gained enough freedom to hope that marriage could at last become more than a master-slave relationship, women failed to know what they wanted marriage to be. And men also failed to provide an answer. The result has been a watering-down of marriage to the point where it is considered a miracle if a marriage relationship brings abiding love and devotion. It is considerably unfashionable to look at marriage with great expectation and idealism.

This is a crucial area of life in which the minister and his wife can add healing through personal application of insight. It is not enough to be good counselors of others; it is imperative to teach by example.

Ministers always have to struggle against the trend of the times in which they live. At times their efforts are heroic and at others simply hard work. Sometimes it is easy to recognize the adversary and to fight him openly; at other times the enemy must be identified before the battle can begin. The invidious attacker of marriage is well hidden. It is important for the minister to find the culprit if only to save his own marriage.

In the first instance, marriage has suffered belittlement at the hands of the enemy. Wherever marriage has been considered a 50-50 proposition, it has been degraded. For it is quite obvious to anyone who has married that to deliver even fifty percent is sometimes downright impossible. Marriage must be a 100-100 percent proposition, for often a husband must support a wife or the wife support the husband in times of failure.

Marriage suffered its severest blow at the hand of the scientific attitude, or what was supposed to be scientific. This resulted in the separation of body, mind, and soul as though each were an entity capable of acting without the consent or involvement of the other. Both promiscuity and prudishness have taken their toll on marriage as a result. The animal pursual of physical desire on the one hand and the prudish rejection of the physical desire as a dirty secret on the other have been equally damaging to wholeness in marriage.

Marriage has suffered great blows because such virtues as self-discipline, trustworthiness and obedience have been replaced by self-expression, and general disregard for anything which curtails personal freedom. Yet it is just these virtues which marriage depends upon for its fullest realization.

The widespread confusion about love has taken its toll. Romantic love has often been the test of marriage rather than married love. Marriage has also suffered by being taken too lightly. The frequent marriages between immature teen-agers testifies to common acceptance of the wedding as something of a game to be played by children.

Yet marriage just barely begins at the altar. Marriage could be described as the commitment to struggle against all odds for oneness. Marriage cannot happen all at once. The exciting thing about it is that it can always be a renewing experience: the perfecting of human relationships is ever-changing.

A minister and his wife are in most favorable circumstances for strengthening marriage. They have the advantages of Christian commitment on their side. They have the Christian concept that the body is not to be despised, nor is it to be worshiped. Increasingly ministers are aware that there is no such thing as a purely physical act. They are gaining new insight into the meaning of married love. For genuine married love involves the whole being in the act of love. The motivation of the act is the giving of love, the receiving of love is incidental. The essential spiritual nature of this most intimate of encounters is expressed in the moment of abandonment of individual identity for oneness. This kind of experience is not bought cheaply: it is truly rare and precious.

A new dimension has been added to marriage by the conscious participation of women as other than coquette or slave-servant. A minister's wife has the distinct advantage of being married to a man who knows how to listen to others. He can, therefore, learn to listen to her as an individual as well as a wife. Revealing the secret places of the heart is a privilege both for the one who would reveal and for the one to whom the secret is made known.

Total acceptance of the married partner for what he or she is is basic to sound marriage. If a wife is acceptable only on the basis that she will certainly improve if given time, she is not really accepted at all. Any partialness in marriage of either commitment or acceptance defeats and endangers stability. Many couples fail in their marriage because one or the other parties sees only what they wish to see in the other. The marriage is sometimes made between people who do not in essence exist, except in the imagination. It is difficult enough for real people to be married; it is impossible for true marriage to exist between the unreal.

One would think that after years and years of marriage there would be no secret places in the partners to be explored. An elderly minister's wife was reminiscing about her married life. She and her husband enjoyed an unusually happy marriage. They even began to look alike as the years rolled by. Yet this wife said, after her husband's death, "I was surprised to learn as I watched my husband during his final hours how little I knew of his inner life. I guess no matter how close you are to another person, nor how much you want to know each other, there are some things which cannot be shared." What a bride of six months cannot accept, a widow after forty years of marriage knows. Beyond all else involved in marriage, it is still a relationship of two individuals. The dignity of a personal identity is not lost in a sound marriage, although it is on occasion surrendered.

If we ponder that ancient phrase so familiar to us in the marriage ceremony in which it is stated that human marriage is to be likened to the mystical union which exists between Christ and his Church, we may be overwhelmed by its implication. When we understand its implication, we will no longer be tempted to take marriage lightly. Perhaps this relationship is more profound than this world imagines, and we have yet to experience it as it can be.

It would be easy for a modern minister to become quite cynical about marriage. He looks around and sees so much heartache in husbands and wives. He is constantly hearing out the complaints of both parties in divorce cases. He deals with the problems of the promiscuous, and he deals with the prudes. The apparently happily married become fewer and fewer as he stays long enough in a parish to know the individuals. His front line of defense against *cynicism* is his own marriage.

A minister's marriage has to endure some challenges not so prevalent in the average marriage. There is the constant stream of lonely, frustrated women to a minister's door. Many of these women are eager for his attention and willing to shower him with their affection. His front line of defense against *temptation* is his own marriage.

A minister may become so exhausted from patching up other people's marriages, he forgets to mend his own walls. There are times in a minister's life when he is simply too weary to contribute much more than his presence to his own marriage. A wife will wisely fill this gap by going the second mile of love and attention. Yet no minister should allow himself the dangerous luxury of always depending upon his wife to keep his marriage warm. He owes his wife some of his best time, attention, and concern, and not always the left-overs when he is too exhausted to help anyone else.

There was a minister who had a wife who did everything wrong. At home she was a miserable housekeeper and didn't know how to entertain gracefully. When she went to church, she talked too much, tried to run things, and generally had a talent for rubbing everyone the wrong way. Yet none of this man's friends ever heard him utter a word against his wife. He may have tried on occasion to improve her, but never in public. He loved her through her errors with a depth of love any woman would have envied. Of course, her redeeming feature was that she also loved him utterly. Theirs was a very special marriage.

Fortunately, all minister's wives are not so thorough in their ineptness. They all fail in some of the areas where they could be of special help to their husbands. Yet the most crucial contribution a wife can possibly make is to love her husband utterly, with complete and abiding loyalty.